AF225794

Shavasana Sun

Taylor Harper

ISBN:

979-8-824-99268-7 (sc)

979-8-810-22742-7 (hc)

Illustrations by Frances Rose Español

Layout and Design by Louie Romares

This book is dedicated to:

All the family members I didn't dedicate the first book to...
Second place isn't bad, right ?

Hi, I'm
Shavasana
Sun!

**Good morning Ruffle
what's the matter?**

That can be very stressful.
Let's try to make it fun.
Repeat after me.

Raise your rooster wings as high as you can while you inhale.

**Now flap flap flap with a
big Cock-A-Doodle-Doo**

Repeat until all the barnyard
animals are awake.

I feel so anxious because
I have to wake everyone
on the farm every morning.

Wow, Dawna, those vegetables look really heavy.

How about we relax
with a hee haw breath?
Follow me!

Hee in for 1,2,3,4
haw out for 1,2,3,4

Carrying all of these vegetables for the farmer has made me tired.

I feel so much better. Thanks, Shavasana!

Why so sad, Pamela?

How about we try to calm them down together?

Alright, everyone follow me.

Breathe in with an oink, oink, oink and out 1,2,3,4,5.

Repeat until all the little piglets are calm.

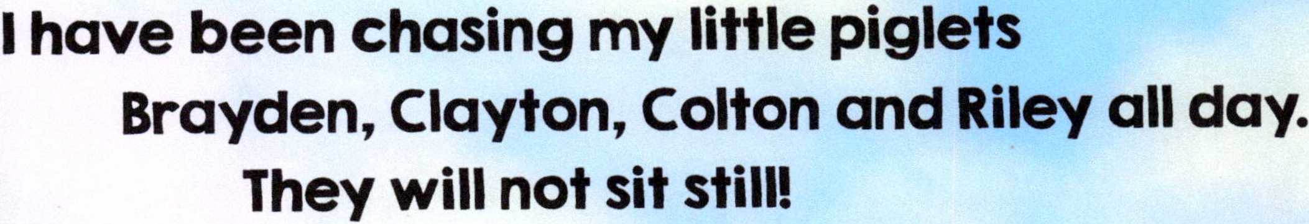

I have been chasing my little piglets
Brayden, Clayton, Colton and Riley all day.
They will not sit still!

Thanks Shavasana,
you really helped.

Connie, it looks like you have a lot of milk!

You know what makes me feel better when I'm stressed ?
Words of affirmation.
Repeat after me: "I am enough. I am enough. I am enough."

I am stressed from providing milk to the farm all day.
I am nervous that I will not make enough.

You are right, Shavasana, I am enough.
I feel so much better.

Why the long face, Henry?
You know what turns my frown upside down when I'm feeling blue? Positive self talk. Repeat after me.

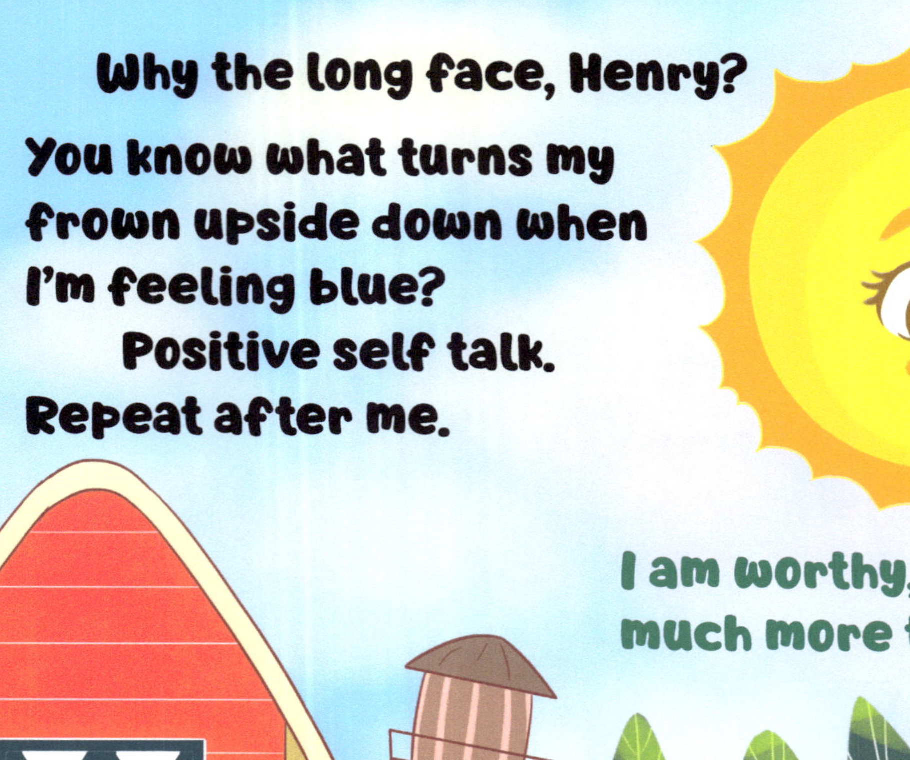

I am worthy, I am enough, I am so much more then my looks.

Repeat until the negative self talk disappears.

All day I trot and look my best. But I don't feel my best inside.
Thanks, Shavasana. I'm so glad I have you as a friend to help when I'm feeling blue.

How are you today, Dalton?

I know just what to do.
Repeat after me.

Breathe in for 1,2,3,4,5,6,7,8,
and let it out with a quack,
quack, quack, quack, quack.

Repeat until you are relaxed.

I've been chasing my ducklings around all day. I need a break.

I feel so much more relaxed.
Time to go chase
after my ducklings.

Hey doodle dogs (Blaze & Benji),
what's the matter?

Let's try to relax.
Repeat after me.

I am a dog sitting as quiet as can be.
I can see all of the things that happen around me.

I take a breath in and let it all be.
Peaceful and still is how you'll find me.

We are so exhausted.
    We have been herding sheep for the farmer all day.

Thanks, Shavasana.
    You really are a good friend.

I have done my best and that
is all I can do.
I hope I helped everyone and
tomorrow we'll start anew.

A Parents Guide to Meditation

Meditation: Is a practice where an individual uses a technique - such as mindfulness, or focusing the mind on a particular object, thought, or activity - to train attention and awareness, and achieve a mentally clear and emotionally calm and stable state.

Mindfulness: A mental state achieved by focusing one's awareness on the present moment, while calmly acknowledging and accepting one's feelings, thoughts, and bodily sensations, used as a therapeutic technique.

Breath work: A New Age term for various breathing practices in which the conscious control of breathing is said to influence a person's mental, emotional or physical state, with a claimed therapeutic effect.

Mantra: A mantra or mantram is a sacred utterance, a numinous sound, a syllable, word or phonemes, or group of words in Sanskrit, Pali and other languages believed by practitioners to have religious, magical or spiritual powers. Some mantras have a syntactic structure and literal meaning, while others do not.

Inner peace: Is defined as the state of physical and spiritual calm despite many stressors. To find your peace of mind means finding happiness, contentment, and bliss no matter how hard you go through in life.

About the Author

Taylor grew up in Chicago where her enthusiasm for mental health and overall wellness flourished. Taylor is a psychologist with a love for inspiring the next generation of readers. She lives in southern California with her husband, son and two fur babies.